THE FACTS ON THE NEW AGE MOVEMENT

John Ankerberg & John Weldon

HARVEST HOUSE PUBLISHERS
Eugene, Oregon 97402

FACTS ON THE NEW AGE MOVEMENT

Copyright © 1988 by Harvest House Publishers
Eugene, Oregon 97402

ISBN 0-89081-711-1

Printed in the United States of America.

PREFACE

The purpose of this booklet is threefold: (1) to provide reliable information in brief and popular language on the New Age Movement; (2) to challenge readers to critically re-examine their own world view; and (3) to express love for those we would like to be our friends by sharing our concerns as to the nature and implications of this topic.

A New Age follower was once quoted in the *New Age Journal* (March, 1978, p. 81) as saying, "I think one of the greatest faults that exists in the spiritual [New Age] movement is that people are not willing to look at what is going on and say maybe it's wrong." We have examined the literature of the New Age Movement in depth and are seeking to give straight answers from the perspective of Biblical revelation, believing that an unbiased examination of the historical, Biblical and logical evidence virtually compels one to acknowledge its truth. No one should be unconcerned about the truth even if it is difficult or unpopular. As Samuel Johnson said, "It is more from carelessness about truth, than from intentional lying that there is so much falsehood in the world."

It is our desire to speak on issues that are complex, and to deal with ultimate questions that are very, very important. Indeed, a correct assessment of these issues may mean the difference between physical or spiritual life and death.

Why? Let us illustrate. A lion is an extremely powerful animal. As long as a lion is caged, it presents no danger to mankind. No man in his right mind would walk into the den of a hungry lion. If he did, he would be seriously injured or killed. Once within the lion's territory, the man would be subject to both the lion's attention and its wishes. In the spiritual world, there is a territory of the lion. It is the realm of the occult. Today unfortunately, men do no believe the lion exists or, if they do, they do not recognize him. Yet men are encroaching upon his realm, drawing his attention, placing themselves at his mercy. The Bible warns, "Be sober, be watchful. Your adversary the devil prowls around like a roaring lion seeking someone to devour." (I Peter 5:8).

At times our brief question-and-answer format has required that we be less detailed than we would wish. For individuals who wish more information, we suggest they consult the recommended reading found at the end of this booklet.

CONTENTS

SECTION IV—Related Philosophies and Issues

SECTION V—Analysis and Critique

Section I

Introduction to the New Age Movement

1. What is the New Age Movement?

Definition: The New Age Movement (NAM) is a title
that refers to a world view or philosophy of life that many
people hold. The NAM can also be properly called a religion
because it is based on religious views; for example, New
Agers hold to pantheism, a belief that everything is a part
of God. That is, God is all, and all is God. They believe that
every man is part of God, even though those outside of the
New Age might not realize it.

Through mystical experiences, or while participating in
techniques which alter one's state of consciousness, people
are powerfully persuaded that the religious world view of
the New Age is true.

An example of this is Shirley MacLaine. During a mystical experience in a hot tub, here is what she said she was led
to believe, "My whole body seemed to float. Slowly, slowly
I **became** the water...I **felt** the inner connection of my
breathing with the pulse of the energy around me. In fact, I
was the air, the water, the darkness, the walls, the bubbles,
the candle, the wet rocks under the water, and even the
sound of the rushing river outside."[1]

Such mystical experiences have led New Agers to believe
they truly are one with the universe and are part of God. It
has also led them to believe they have uncovered "human
potential," an alleged divine power within themselves that,
they think, exists in all men. New Agers want to help
everybody discover this power and experientially realize
they are one with God. Once people have the mystical experience, New Agers expect that people will live out their new
world view. This would mean striving for world unity and
peace and then using their new powers to bring it about.

Many New Agers describe encounters with spirit guides or spirit beings. These spirit beings depict themselves as good spirits who claim to be people who have died and now reside in the spirit world to guide and help others spiritually.

The New Ager's interpretation of these mystical experiences, higher consciousness, spirit beings, etc., differs from the interpretations of orthodox Christianity. Orthodox Christianity has come to the conclusion that New Agers have embraced a mixture of Eastern religious beliefs along with many forms of the occult, such as "channeling," or spirit-possession. It is our belief that the dramatic out-of-the-body experiences, extra-sensory knowledge, and the mind trips given to New Agers during their altered states of consciousness are typically experiences given by demons to fool people into believing New Age philosophy.

For example, people in hospitals sometimes see huge rats or pink elephants that scare them. No one doubts they are really seeing these things, but the visions are a false reality. Likewise, the demons can give wonderful visions and experiences in order to fool people into believing a false religious view of the world. That these beings are evil spirits can be documented from psychology, history, religion and the experience of many New Agers.

In I Timothy 4:1 we read, "The Spirit clearly says that in the later time some will abandon the faith and follow deceiving spirits and things taught by demons."

In John 8:44 Jesus stated, "The devil . . . is a liar and the father of lies."

In II Corinthians 11:14 we read "For Satan himself masquerades as an angel of light."

In brief, orthodox Christianity views the New Age Movement as a false religious world view, motivated and taught by Satan's demons masquerading as benevolent spirit guides concerned with the welfare of humanity.

2. Why is the New Age Movement important?

The New Age Movement is important because of its current potential for influence at all levels of society—in education, health, psychology, the arts, business, industry, government, religion, science, and entertainment.[2]

According to Marilyn McGuire, Executive Director of the New Age Publishing and Retailing Alliance, there are some 2,500 occult bookstores in the U.S. and over 3,000 publishers of occult books and journals.[3] Sales of New Age books in particular are estimated at $1 billion a year.[4] This makes the New Age Movement a multi-billion-dollar industry, and such industries receive the attention of corporate America and those in power.

Famous entertainers are being influenced by the New Age and they in turn influence many people in America. Helen Reddy, Marsha Mason, Lisa Bonet, Tina Turner, and musician Paul Horn are only a few of the entertainment industry's New Age converts.[5] Shirley MacLaine's books and televised mini-series "Out on a Limb" introduced millions of people to New Age occultism and spirit contact.

Many other famous personalities have appeared on Phil Donahue, Oprah Winfrey and other major talk shows endorsing spirit guides and/or the New Age. Entity-channel teams, comprised of mediums and their spirit guides, have become local and national radio and television personalities. For example, on July 25, 1986, actor and convert Michael York appeared on the Merv Griffin Show with Jach Pursel who channeled "Lazaris" before an audience of millions. Merv Griffin himself commented "many of our top stars are now consulting the entity" ("Lazaris"). Actress Sharon Gless who plays "Cagney" on the hit TV series "Cagney and Lacey" won a 1987 "Emmy" for her role on the series. In her acceptance speech, she told tens of millions that her success was due to "Lazaris." Linda Evans of "Dynasty" fame and Joyce DeWitt (formerly of "Three's Company") follow the guidance of another spirit being, "Mafu," channeled by housewife Penny Torres.[6]

Occult filmstrips are promoting seances and necromancy (contacting the dead) in some elementary schools;[7] Tarot card readings are offered at a McDonald's Restaurant;[8] university students are turning out by the thousands to hear guest lectures on the occult.[9] There is also a new faith emerging in "scientific mysticism," or the mixture of the occult and science, and occultic New Age themes are impacting many sectors of society.[10]

In brief the NAM is important because it is shifting the way Americans think away from Judeo-Christian values to the practices of the occult.

3. Who are some of the leaders in the New Age Movement?

Shirley MacLaine is the most visible of New Age proponents; her televised mini-series reached millions and apparently inspired thousands to take up channeling. Her

1987 nationwide seminars were attended by some 14,000 people.[11] She has begun a 300-acre spiritistic retreat center in Crestone, Colorado that will make channelers (those whom spirits speak through) available for any and all visitors.[12] Although she rejects the title of leader or guru, the *Los Angeles Times Magazine* titled her "the super sales woman for a fast growing New Age Movement."[13]

A brief listing of some New Age notables would include New Age theorist and "transpersonal" psychologist, Ken Wilbur, dubbed by some "the Einstein of consciousness research,"[14] ("transpersonal" psychology seeks for example, to blend Eastern religion and modern psychology[15]).

Medium Ruth Montgomery was once a tough-minded journalist who was an agnostic. She converted to the New Age and became a major popularizer of its teachings. She has now written books on the New Age, UFOs, contacting the dead, and related subjects. Marilyn Ferguson is one of the spiritual leaders of the New Age and wrote the best selling book *The Aquarian Conspiracy: Personal and Social Transformation in the 1980's*. She is also editor of the *Brain-Mind Bulletin* and the *Leading Edge Bulletin* which discuss the scientific and social advances of the New Age.

Other influential New Agers include Werner Erhard, founder of est (Erhard Seminars Training), Fritjof Capra, a physicist who is author of the New Age texts, *The Tao of Physics* and *The Turning Point*, and Carlos Castaneda, a UCLA anthropology student whose studies led him into the occult. He is the author of the multi-million-selling series of books on sorcery, such as *The Teachings of Don Juan: A Yaqui Way of Knowledge*. Benjamin Creme is the self proclaimed forerunner of a New Age guru, Maitreya. He is also author of *The Reappearance of the Christ and the Masters of Wisdom*. John Lilly and Charles Tart are pioneering scientific researchers of altered states of consciousness, and Robert Muller, Assistant to the Secretary General of the United Nations, is the author of *New Genesis: Shaping a Global Spirituality*.

There are several major institutions of the New Age. One is Esalen in Big Sur, California. It appears as if almost every major figure in the New Age has been to Esalen or been influenced by it.[16] Another major institution would be the many New Age publishers, such as Shambala of Boston and J. P. Tarcher of Los Angeles, who are providing the intellectual underpinning for the New Age. Famous New Age doctors include Norman Shealy, author of *Occult Medicine Can Save Your Life*; Robert Leightman, who "channels" many of the famous dead, and mystic W. Brugh Joy, author of *Joy's Way*. World renowned gurus of the NAM include Bhagwan Shree Rajneesh, Swami Muktananda, and Sri Aurobindo among others.

Although there are scores of influential human guides of the New Age Movement, it is the spirit world, over the last two decades, which has provided the groundwork and the most potent leadership behind the scenes. These spirits have, through human agents, produced hundreds of texts with millions of copies of their books in print. Two modern mediums in particular may be considered important catalysts for the current revival of "spirit-written" books. In the 1960's and the 1970's both Jane Roberts and Ruth Montgomery crossed over to the large publishing houses. Between them, their two spirit guides, "Seth" and "Lilly" respectively, have penned almost thirty texts for several major publishers. They not only broke the mold, they set a trend. When Richard Bach's *Jonathan Livingston Seagull* (also dictated by an entity) broke all publishing records since *Gone With the Wind* and made the best-seller list for over two years, the die was cast. Over 25 million copies of the book have been sold worldwide. Today, the sheer number of titles of "spirit-written" books in print is unprecedented.

4. What are the basic beliefs of the New Age world view?

The NAM can be summarized in four basic beliefs: 1) that all true reality is divine ("God is all; all is God"); 2) that personal "enlightenment" is important (since men exist in a state of ignorance as to their divine nature); 3) that altered consciousness, psychic powers, and spirit contact are the means of such enlightenment; and 4) that in many quarters social and political activism is needed to help "network" (organize) people of like mind to produce a united world—socially, economically, religiously, and politically.

While there are wide variations of belief in the New Age, there is a broad consensus on the main points: the nature of God (God is impersonal), man (man is part of God), the predicament of man (ignorance of his divine nature), and the solution to human problems (accepting New Age beliefs and practices).

The basic New Age world view that "all is God" is why actress Shirley MacLaine could stand before the Pacific Ocean, arms outstretched and chant, "I am God, I am God, I am God."[17] This is why the Eastern gurus claim they are God—and so is everyone else. For example, guru Sathya Sai Baba states that "... you are the God of this universe."[18]

5. What moral consequences logically follow to anyone holding a New Age world view?

Believing that everything is God does have consequences; however, we have space for only one illustration. In the area of morality, the NAM world view is an occultic view which teaches that evil is really an illusion and that belief in an absolute morality is wrong. This is why guru Bhagwan Shree Rajneesh states: "I don't believe in morality" and "I am bent on destroying it;" "to emphasize morality is mean, degrading, it is inhuman."[19] Since God is all in Eastern thinking, He includes both good and evil. Since God is impersonal, He therefore cannot be concerned over right or wrong. Thus, whatever is, is right. In fact, once a person realizes and accepts his own godhood, then by definition whatever he does is good, even if it is evil. This is why Rajneesh again states, "My ashram [spiritual community] makes no difference between the demonic and the divine."[20] This is why Swami Vivekananda can say, "Good and evil are one and the same."[21] Although the Bible teaches "Thou shalt not kill" (Exodus 20:13), Swami Vivekananda says, "The murderer too is God."[22] And Rajneesh even says, explaining the Bhagavad Gita (a Hindu holy book), "Kill, murder, fully conscious, knowing that no one is murdered and no one is killed."[23]

Thus we see how the basic world view of the NAM ("all is one") is able to pervert so important a topic as moral values. Although many other areas could be discussed, we mention that the New Age world view is also a comprehensive world view. New Agers want to reinterpret all fields of knowledge to harmonize with New Age belief, including physics, psychology, biology, religion, and sociology. The reason for this is because their mystical experiences have persuaded them this is necessary, not only because these mystical experiences have revealed the "true" interpretation of these disciplines but because this will help educate people toward New Age thinking. This is why their library consists of revelations from the spirit world on these subjects.[24]

For example, these spirits teach that true science is both material and spiritual because of such things as ESP, and psychic healing. The science of parapsychology (the scientific study of the occult) helps to align the general sciences with Eastern and occult views.

The bottom line here is that there are very few areas the NAM leaves untouched.

6. Why are nonreligious people embracing this new religious view? (Scientists, atheists, rationalists, etc.)

One reason is that regardless of personal belief, men are nevertheless spiritual beings created in the image of God (Genesis 1:27; Ecclesiastes 3:11). As such, they require some kind of spiritual reality to provide a true basis for meaning to life.

An illustration of how non-religious scientists may become disenchanted with science and open the doors to New Age religion is found in Stanislav Grof's text, *Ancient Wisdom and Modern Science*, where leading scientists have blended modern science with ancient occultism.[25] This text and many like it reveal that hundreds of scientists and academics are leaning toward the New Age. Also many of them admit they have turned to Eastern gurus and/or have become practicing disciples of various occult traditions. These scientists have joined the NAM because they are attracted to the New Age idea of an inner divine potential within man and because they see "proof" of this in the occult power they are experiencing. These scientists say they cannot find meaning in life through a purely material science, and they choose not to investigate it in Christianity, but they believe they have found this meaning in the NAM. As a result they have integrated science with occultism leading to an Eastern religious view of reality. In the process they have distorted science and made it a religion. For example, some leading scientists now state that because of their conversion to the NAM, they have changed their mind as to the nature of the universe. What they once believed was a real world is now seen as an illusion. What they used to think was an illusion (occult views of the universe) is now seen as a reality. It is this "reality" which they intend to investigate.[25a]

7. What are mystical experiences?

Mystical experiences are very important in the New Age Movement, especially because they tend to confirm New Age beliefs. In the New Age, mystical experiences are most frequently induced by human means (yoga, meditation, drug use) or by means of contact with spirits. A mystical experience usually involves a misperception of physical or spiritual reality.

For those who aren't already believers in an Eastern world view, the mystical experiences are important because they seem to bring all the proof that is needed to persuade. Thus, in the NAM the mystical experience conclusively persuades that "all is God" and "God is all," and that men can tap a reservoir of inner divine power. Besides the feelings of the divine oneness of all things, common mystical experience involves a feeling of going beyond matter, time, and space which is often perceived as illusion. Mystical experiences also produce various behavior and attitude changes that reflect New Age beliefs. In addition the experience of spirits or unusual energies is common.[26]

From a Biblical point of view, these experiences are dangerous and to be avoided because they lead people to contact the spirit world, to believe in occult philosophy, and to develop psychic abilities. They may also lead to spirit possession. These experiences cause people to wrongly believe they are inwardly God. As such they prevent faith in Christ as Savior and cannot be divine, no matter how divine they appear.

Section II
New Age Practices and Goals

8. What are some of the "new" occult techniques and practices of the New Age Movement?

There are hundreds of different practices in the NAM such as meditation, channeling, psychic healing, the use of "magical" objects, and various "holistic" therapies such as acupressure, homeopathy, etc. There are scores of cults and new "therapies" which also use these practices. The Rajneesh sect alone uses dozens of different methods to attain its goals of drastically changing human consciousness.

These practices have been developed from the teachings of many ancient cultures and may have been blended with the exercises of modern occultism. In addition, recent developments in psychology, technology, and medicine offer the NAM new options for altering consciousness (such as biofeedback).

In this booklet we have room to discuss only two of the most popular New Age practices, both of which are related to spiritism; channeling and using crystals as sources of occult power.

9. What is channeling?

Channeling is a New Age term for spirit possession where a willing human "channel" or medium relinquishes his mind and body to an invading spirit who then possesses and controls that person for its own purposes, usually as a mouthpiece to give the spirit's own teachings. Some of the more prominent spirits with current nationwide influence are "Lazaris," "Mafu," "Seth," "Saint Germain," and "Ramtha."[27] Over all, it can be documented there are hundreds of spirits claiming responsibility for New Age books and their message has reached millions of people. In Los Angeles alone there are now an estimated one thousand channelers.[28] (For an analysis of the nature of these spirits, see Q. 26).

Major spiritistic revivals are not new in America; for example, they occurred in 1848 and in 1876. Judging from the tens of thousands who have taken up this practice in recent years, we are currently in the early stages of another revival. Thus, spiritism has become big business. New Age educator and psychologist, Jon Klimo, observes that "cases of channeling have become pervasive." Scores of new and old chaneled books are being rushed to print, numerous guide books exist for spirit contact;[29] new magazines such as *Spirit Speaks* are devoted solely to channeled revelations,[30] and profits from channeled seminars, tapes, and books alone range from 100 million to 400 million dollars a year.[31]

For example, Jach Pursel channels "Lazaris" (the entity unexpectedly possessed him one evening during meditation and began speaking through him). A weekend seminar with "Lazaris" (through Pursel) will cost $275 per person with 600 to 800 people in attendance or $200,000 per weekend. At almost $100 per hour for a private sitting, "Lazaris" still has a two-year waiting list; his audio tapes sell at $20 per set, video tapes at $60. "Lazaris" may also be contacted by phone at $53 per half hour charged to your Mastercard or Visa.[32]

A recent prestigious poll reported that 67% of Americans now believe in the supernatural, and that 42% "believe they have been in contact with someone who died."[33] Thus the stage has been set for a revival of spiritism that could dwarf earlier eras. Some have asserted that channeling will one day be "bigger than fundamentalism."[34] Regardless, spirit contact has become in many quarters a socially acceptable practice—and the spirits have served notice that they intend to influence our future.

10. How has channeling influenced even the church?

Spiritism has, unfortunately, influenced the church. Many professing Christians fail to see anything wrong or unchristian in channeling. For example, Laura Cameron Fraser, the first woman Episcopal priest of the Pacific Northwest, chose to resign as rector of her church rather than renounce her faith in a channeled spirit named "Jonah."[35]

To cite one of many illustrations of such influence in the church, a number of spiritistically-produced texts have ignorantly been accepted by some Christians because they sound spiritual or claim to be inspired by God or Jesus. These include the devotional text *God Calling* (Revell publishers, edited by A. J. Russell) which has been on the evangelical best-seller list for almost two years now.[36] Many others are surprised to discover that Richard Bach's *Jonathan Livingston Seagull* was also on the evangelical best-seller list, in spite of its Eastern teachings. It was also inspired by supernatural sources.[37] Another illustration is the three-volume *A Course In Miracles*. This text by Helen Schucman has sold in the hundreds of thousands and has recently found an interested and expanding audience within Christianity.[38] Both *God Calling* and *A Course In Miracles* claim to be written by either God or Jesus, which is impossible because they deny the Biblical Jesus and contradict the Bible.

The most obvious reason for Christian acceptance of such material is the fact that Biblical ignorance and worldliness are common among Christians. The church is failing to educate her people properly in these areas.

11. What dangerous potential lies ahead for America if we continue to follow "channelers"?

If the trend continues, the spirits could, through human mediums, offer actual classes on television and video tapes. The more powerful "channelers" would have live trance interviews or be "taped-in-trance" and the material played back on educational television or through other media. To millions of Americans the spirits are already accepted as "wise," instructive and as entertaining as human teachers. If hundreds of millions of dollars are now being spent to listen to spirits on cassette and video, this means the age of electronic spirit contact is already here. If there is a large enough audience and sales potential, television programs offering the spirits as "entertainment" may not be far off.

Even the spirits themselves are actively promoting the idea of "educational" spiritism. Consider the following statement by the spirit being called "Mentor" who speaks through Meredith Lady Young. The spirit has reached thousands through mediumistic seminars conducted before large audiences. Ms. Young stated that "Mentor" told her "it will not be long, 50 years perhaps, before 'channeling' will be considered the norm rather than the exception . . . humankind will enter the New Age of awareness, learning to integrate the mystical and the practical. One's 'teachers' or 'spirit guides' will be as common as one's professors at a university. The professor will teach mathematics and the spiritual 'teacher' will enlighten."[39]

12. Why are crystals being used by New Agers?

New Agers believe their impersonal God exists as an Energy that is vibrating everywhere in the universe. If one wants to get into harmony with this energy, New Agers believe they may do so through certain objects that vibrate in harmony with God. We are all familiar with the TV commercials in which the singer hits a high note and the sound waves vibrate a crystal glass and break it. New Agers believe crystal rocks vibrate to the energy patterns of God and can help a person feel and use this energy. New Agers have found that by meditating and holding crystals or being in their presence sometimes powers are released. One major use involves the alleged focusing or directing of crystal energy for specific purposes, such as psychic healing, contact with spirits, or developing higher consciousness and psychic powers.

In essence, New Age crystal use is the modern equivalent of what missionaries deal with in occultic societies— the practice of using magic charms and other occultic objects believed to possess supernatural power for either good or evil use.

These objects themselves have no power. However, when used for occult purposes, they can become vehicles for spirits to work through, much like common wood (divining rod, Ouija board), cards or sticks (Tarot cards, I Ching).

13. Are New Age beliefs and practices really based on spiritism?

To put it simply, the teachings of the New Age are the teachings of the spirits. What the New Age teaches and believes is what the spirit world has revealed and wishes men to believe. Many of the practices are also based upon instructions received from the spirit world. In other words, the New Age teachings and practices are not simply the enlightened discoveries of men, but more precisely the deliberately revealed teachings of the spirits that men have adopted and utilized. They merely appear to be enlightened teachings because the spirits use psychological principles and spiritual language; they speak of God and love; and they satisfy many of the genuine desires of fallen men. They provide practices which confirm the truth of the New Age world view to the individual convert. Nevertheless, the spirits have given such teachings and practices for the express purpose of deceiving men under the pretense of loving God and helping men evolve spiritually toward "their true destiny." The Bible is clear at this point; there are teachings given to man by deceitful spirits and they influence both the church and society.

> **"But the Spirit clearly says that in later times some will abandon the faith, and follow deceitful spirits and things taught by demons" (I Timothy 4:1).**

> **"And no wonder, for even Satan himself masquerades as an angel of light" (II Corinthians 11:14).**

The spirits are coming out of the closet in force, in numerous disguises, doing all they can to spread the teachings of the New Age and similar themes. Again, this is often their stated purpose—to help mankind usher in "the New Age."

Yet these spirits are in fact the personal, malevolent spirit beings that the Bible classifies as "unclean spirits" or demons. It is they who are the underlying power behind "modern" New Age practices and teachings. The basic reason that people cannot bring themselves to accept this conclusion is because the spirits disguise their motives and deceptively appear as good and friendly beings. Thus, most persons trust the spirits' claims about themselves. In return they receive blessings from them in the form of exciting revelations, blissful experiences, loving encounters, help and encouragement, protection from dangers, and endless assurances about their own divinity (not to mention their lack of need for repentance and faith in the Biblical Jesus Christ).

Section III

The Theology of the New Age

14. What are the religious beliefs of the New Age Movement?

In general, the religious views of the NAM are:

- God—an impersonal all-pervading energy.
- The Holy Spirit—an energy that can be used creatively or psychically.
- Jesus Christ—a New Age teacher and illustration of an enlightened individual who realized he was God.
- Man—inwardly good and divine; thus he carries within himself all that he needs for time and eternity.
- Salvation—development of psychic powers and higher consciousness. This is achieved by looking inside one's self and practicing New Age techniques to finally attain awareness of personal divinity.
- Sin—ignorance of personal divinity.
- Death—the moment one hopes to experience a merging with God, the all pervading energy of the universe. This only comes if personal transformation or enlightenment has been obtained.
- Satan—normal consciousness—man existing in his state of unrealized potential.
- Heaven—Hell—good or bad states of consciousness in this life.

In the New Age, God is impersonal and is one and the same as the universe. Technically, many in the NAM believe in pantheism.[40] In Christianity, God is the personal Creator who is separate, distinct, and over His Creation. In the New Age, man is only a part of an impersonal God. As such, man shares God's essential nature. In Christianity, however, God specifically created man other than himself. Because of man's rebellion against God, he is separated from Him. According to the New Age, man must transform himself. He does this by changing his consciousness and actualizing his divine nature. In doing so he becomes aware of his inner divinity. According to Christianity, Jesus Christ alone is the Savior and reconciles man to God. In the New Age, salvation is by personal effort and works. Man must use a variety of Eastern or occultic techniques and apply these to his mind, body, and spirit to obtain enlightenment. In Christianity, salvation is by God's grace and not by man's work. Man must receive God's gift by placing his faith in Christ and turning from sin. Salvation is not something earned by personal merit. (Eph. 2:8-9)

15. Does the Bible say anything about the teachings and practices of the New Age Movement?

The Bible has much to say about the practices and teachings of the NAM. Specifically, the Bible teaches that spiritism and other occult practices of the NAM are displeasing to God, inviting his judgment; for example:

> **Exodus 20:3 (cf. Ps. 96:4)—"You shall have no other gods before me. You shall not bow down or worship them...."**

> **Deut. 18:9-12 (cf. II Chron. 33:6)—"Let no one be found among you... who practices divination, or sorcery, interprets omens, engages in witchcraft, or one who casts spells, or who is a medium, or spiritist, or who consults the dead. Anyone who does these things is detestable to the Lord..."**

> **I Cor. 10:20 (cf. Ps. 106:34-40)—"the sacrifices... are offered to demons, not to God, and I do not want you to be participants with demons."**

In essence in these verses the Bible is condemning any involvement with spirits or demons.

The pantheistic teachings of the NAM are rejected by Scripture. The Bible teaches that the eternal infinite God created a finite universe from nothing (Gen. 1:1; Neh. 9:6; Ps. 33:9; 148:5; Heb. 11:3) and that it is both real and good (Gen. 1:31). God is not "one" with the universe (Is. 45:18, 22). He is separate and over it.

The Bible teaches that both wisdom and knowledge come by non-mystical means (Prov. 1; I Tim. 4:10-16; II Timothy 2:15; 3:14) and rejects the New Age idea that so-called "higher" knowledge is available in mystical states of consciousness. Revealed knowledge of God and spiritual truth come from God himself who is Truth, who "cannot lie" (John 14:6; Titus 1:2), by means of verifiable divine revelation (II Tim. 3:16-17), not spiritistic imitations that give false information (I Tim. 4:1; I John 4:1).

The Bible teaches an absolute morality that is based on God's character and His revealed Word (I John 1:5; 2:29; 3:4). This rejects the NAM teaching of a morality based on personal preference which can lead to a potentially destructive approach to personal living and ethics.

Concerning knowledge of God, the Bible teaches that God is infinite (I Kings 8:27; I Timothy 6:15-16), personal (Isaiah 43:10-13; 44:6-9), loving (I John 4:8), holy and immutable (Psalm 55:19; Malachi 3:6; Hebrews 13:8; James 1:17). On the other hand, the NAM teaches that God is impersonal, and therefore should properly be referred to as an "It" like the "Force" in the Star Wars movies. The NAM God cannot love, is not holy, and cannot think, or be merciful. "It" just is.

The Bible teaches that Christ was unique in nature as the only incarnation of God and the Savior of the world (John 3:16,18; Philippians 2:1-8; I John 2:2). He will return visibly and personally (Matthew 24:29-38; Acts 1:11). The Bible rejects the NAM teaching that Christ was merely an enlightened master or spirit guide.

The Bible teaches that sin is real (I John 1:8-10), that sin separates an individual from God (Isaiah 59:2; Revelation 20:12,15), and that Christ died to forgive human sin (John 3:16; I Peter 2:24). This contrasts with the NAM which teaches that sin is an illusion (or mere ignorance of one's own perfection) and that Christ did not die for sin, but merely revealed the way to higher consciousness.

In the Bible salvation occurs when a man repents and receives by faith Christ's provision for his sin. Salvation is an instantaneous free gift received by grace through faith in the sacrificial death of Jesus Christ (Romans 11:6; Ephesians 2:8-9; John 6:47; I John 2:25; 5:13). This rejects the

NAM view that salvation ("enlightenment") is a lengthy process of realizing one's own divinity. This is not a gift, but is achieved by personal effort and merit as in yoga meditation. The Bible teaches a real heaven or hell is the destination for all individuals after their lifetime (Matthew 25:46; Philippians 3:20,21; Hebrews 9:27; Revelation 20:10-15; 21:1–22:5). This rejects the NAM teaching of reincarnation throughout endless numbers of lifetimes. Thus, the Bible and the NAM disagree on many basic beliefs about God, salvation and the spiritual life.

16. Do New Age writers use Christian words and refer to Jesus Christ and the Bible?

The NAM does use Christian words, does refer to Jesus Christ and quotes Bible verses, but this does not make it Christian. In fact it is anti-Christian. Merely using Christian words is no guarantee that Christian definitions are being given to those words. The words in the Bible come to us fixed and clearly defined by their cultural setting. The New Age redefines Biblical words to fit its own ideas and so distorts their intended meaning. As a result, the New Age does not allow the Bible to speak for itself.

The same is true for many groups which outwardly appear Christian, yet whose teachings are not; for example, Jehovah's Witnesses, the Church of Jesus Christ of Latter-Day Saints [Mormonism], the World Wide Church of God [Armstrongism], The Way International [Victor Paul Wierwille], the Unification Church [Sun Myung Moon] and others.[41]

It should also be pointed out that the NAM which offers a sincere, although distorted, view of Christianity in some quarters offers the persecution of Christians in other quarters. A thorough reading of New Age literature will show that some New Agers sanction the persecution of Christians. They do so on the basis of the need to remove those who may refuse to accept or attempt to "prevent" a spiritual uniting of humanity.[42] This is one of the darker aspects to the New Age, yet it is consistent with the overall world view of the NAM. If true globalism—or world unity—is eventually to be a reality, then by definition all dissenting voices must either be converted, silenced, or removed. That, of course, is the "rub"—the New Age of love and harmony may have to be repressive for a time to usher in their version of peace on earth.

Nevertheless, we wish to carefully emphasize the following: First, that not all New Agers are advocating the persecution of Christians. Second, that unfortunately, there are some parts of the NAM which do.

17. Why are some in the New Age antagonistic to Christianity?

Given the teachings of the NAM, the rejection of Christianity is quite logical, although not all in the New Age are openly hostile to the Christian faith. Indeed, many members come from nominal Christian backgrounds or are liberal Christians and for this reason are seeking to combine Christianity and the New Age. Nevertheless, there are those who have openly asserted that it was their dislike for orthodox Christian faith which led them into the New Age. As with certain secular philosophies, they found the NAM attractive simply because it rejected Christian faith and promoted freedom from the Christian God. In addition, some who are fanatically committed to the NAM and are also familiar with Christian teachings are openly antagonistic to Christianity because they realize that the Christian faith is a formidable barrier to New Age views ("all is one," spiritual evolution, salvation by personal merit, etc.) and to New Age goals (occult enlightenment, globalism, etc.). This is why Rajneesh, for example, says that "the greatest deception is the deception of devotion to God."[43] He recognizes that belief in the Christian God is harmful to his own interests. These individuals have labeled Christianity an "enemy" of mankind and in the tradition of those like the founder of the Theosophical Society, Helena P. Blavatsky, have attacked and ridiculed it. They do so, because like the Marxist of today, they recognize the Christian faith for the genuine threat that it is.

18. How can we tell that the New Age is influencing the Christian church?

We have already seen that some Christians are purchasing spiritistic books in large numbers (why Christian publishers would print and distribute such books in the first place is hard to fathom). Christians are also dabbling in various forms of mysticism, Eastern meditation and religion, parapsychology, visualization and positive thinking, and other New Age practices. For example, few Christians know that Napoleon Hill's book *Grow Rich With Peace of*

Mind came from the "Ascended Masters" or spirit beings. Hill said that unseen spirits hovered about him and claimed that the "Ascended Masters" gave him the materials in the chapters of his book.[44] Hill joined with Clement Stone and co-authored a book using the same philosophy to develop the idea of a positive mental attitude known as PMA. Norman Vincent Peale picked up parts of New Age philosophy (which can be seen in some of his books[45]) and, through evangelical "positive thinkers," these ideas have come into the church.

It is interesting that even positive thinker Robert Schuller advocates a form of Eastern meditation which brings a person into the "alpha state." He also discusses the benefits of Eastern mantras.[46]

The influence of the NAM among Christians can also be seen in an issue of *Yoga Journal*. In that issue two persons who claim to be Christians, practice "yoga, T'ai Chi and akido" and state that Christians "stand to gain by learning discipline and spiritual awareness from the East" and the NAM. These men discuss their Eastern "introspective" form of meditation where they have learned to look within "to discover spiritual realities." They have taught two-month seminars on this meditation (which they claim is Christian) at their "conservative evangelical church" and they offer seminars on such meditation at other Christian churches.[47]

Another example is therapist E.S. Gallegos who works at a Lutheran Family Service counseling center and is co-author of *Inner Journeys: Visualization In Growth And Therapy.* He offers the church a therapy incorporating occult theory and technique (shamanism) with visualization and modern psychology.[48]

Finally we may note that parapsychology (the scientific study of the occult) is influencing the Christian church in a variety of ways. For example, a major Christian text on psychology gives qualified endorsement to such topics as psychic healing, parapsychology, and automatic writing.[49]

19. Why is Christianity susceptible to New Age ideas?

Christians are being influenced by the NAM principally because of ignorance of Biblical teachings and lack of doctrinal knowledge. Because of America's emphasis on materialism, commitment to Christ as Lord in every area of life is sadly lacking. This brings disastrous results. Unfortunately there are Christians who "love the approval of men rather than God" (John 12:43); who integrate the world's ways with their Christian faith (James 1:27; I John 2:15; 4:4) or who are ignorant of the extent of spiritual warfare (Acts 20:28-34; II Corinthians 4:4; Ephesians 6:12-18; II Peter 2:1; I John 4:1-3).

These sins of American Christianity open us to false philosophy such as the NAM. There are always some Christians who will actively embrace their culture. Whether they attempt to learn from it intellectually or borrow from it spiritually, or relish the enjoyment of worldly pleasures and pastimes, or attempt some kind of social reform along nominal Christian lines, the result is that their Christian faith becomes diluted or absorbed by an initially appealing but alien culture. This means that to the extent America turns to the New Age, to some degree there will be Christians who will adopt New Age practices or beliefs.

20. What can concerned persons do about the New Age Movement?

The church needs to have a higher degree of commitment to Christ as Lord in every area of life, to studying and living the Bible's teachings, and to learning apologetics (Christian evidences). We need to take sanctification (growth in obedience to Christ) more seriously, recognizing that because the world's ways are so ungodly the Bible warns us, "friendship with the world is enmity toward God. Therefore whosoever will be a friend of the world is the enemy of God" (James 4:4).

As a Christian, this is what you personally can do. First, you can become informed about the New Age (see recommended reading). Secondly, you can "contend earnestly for the faith which was once for all delivered to the saints" (Jude 3) and "sanctify Christ as Lord in your hearts, always being ready to make a defense to everyone who asks you to give an account for the hope that is in you, yet with gentleness and reverence" (I Peter 3:15). You can "examine everything carefully" and actively critique what is not sound, being "wise in what is good, and innocent in what is evil" (I Thessalonians 5:23; Romans 16:19). Thirdly, you can effectively prepare for spiritual warfare (Ephesians 6:10-18) and use the Bible intelligently, "for the Word of God is living and active and sharper than any two-edged sword, and piercing as far as the division of soul and spirit... and able to judge the thoughts and intents of the heart" (Hebrews 4:12). You can also encourage your pastor to speak forcefully about these issues from the Bible.

How can you deal with your friends who have joined the NAM? First you need to realize that you are not just dealing with man's philosophies which can be countered with human arguments. You are dealing with demonic deceptions that require prayer, patience, and the Word of God. These false philosophies and practices will have the devil's power behind them, which is why they cannot be effectively defeated by human means alone. Thus, you should meet these problems with earnest prayer, which "can accomplish much" (James 5:16), with patience and courage (Joshua 1:7; II Timothy 2:24-26), and with the power of the Holy Spirit and the Word of God. You should also love others and be careful to respect those who disagree with you, for in this way you will prove to the world you are truly a disciple of Christ (John 13:35; I Corinthians 10:24,33; 13:13).

Section IV

Related Philosophies and Issues

21. Is holistic health related to the New Age Movement?

The holistic health movement may be considered the "medical" arm of the NAM. The ideas of the NAM have invaded the medical world through a variety of unsound and/or potentially occultic practices such as Applied Kinesiology ("muscle testing"), Homeopathy (a diluting of certain essences for medical treatment), Iridology (the alleged medical diagnosis by inspection of the iris), Therapeutic Touch (an Eastern form of "laying on of hands"), and dozens of other unproven treatments.[50]

In general, most holistic therapies are unscientific in nature and as such potentially dangerous when it comes to life-threatening illness. Using a treatment that has no power to cure can be deadly in the wrong situations. What then about reports of genuine cures? The reports of genuine cures are not so much related to the individual "treatments" used; rather, many times it totally depends on the psychological factors involved. Finally, it must not be forgotten that some treatments work because of the occult power behind them.

How can one tell if a treatment is occult or based on true medicine? The basic question one should ask is whether or not a given practice can be scientifically replicated or whether it is just another form of mystical experience.

In *New Age Medicine*, authors Paul Reisser, M.D., Terri Reisser, and John Weldon list the following important cautions about New Age medical practices: beware of therapies which claim to manipulate "invisible energy"; beware of those who seem to utilize psychic knowledge or power;

beware of a practitioner who has a therapy with which no one else is familiar; beware of someone who claims that his or her particular therapy will cure anything; beware of someone whose explanations do not make sense; beware of therapies whose only proof consists of the testimonies of satisfied customers; beware of therapies which rely heavily on altered states of consciousness; and finally realize that sincerity is no guarantee of legitimacy.[51]

22. What is parapsychology?

Parapsychology is the scientific study of occult phenomena. Parapsychologists study such things as mediumism, poltergeists or "troublesome ghosts," and psychic healing. The claims made by many parapsychologists that they do not study occultic phenomena are basically false. An examination of the literature in the field, including the publication and research reports of the scientific laboratories reveal that parapsychologists study occult phenomena although they may redefine it in more neutral or scientific terms. In fact, for 130 years mediumism has been the mainstay of parapsychology, even within periods of lessened interest in that particular subject. God's warning in Deuteronomy 18 applies to both the professional and non-professional investigator of occult phenomena.[52]

23. Is there a New Age conspiracy to control the world?

An examination of New Age writings reveals that many in the NAM have as their goals: (1) a one-world government; (2) a one-world economic system; (3) a one-world culture, where all education, religion, and races are joined in harmony and (4) a god-like world ruler who will help to implement these changes.[53] What makes these ideas desirable is that the world is fragmented by regional wars and nationalism, by competing ideologies such as Marxism and capitalism, by races, by various monetary standards, and by many conflicting world religions. Thus, it is the hopelessness of the world that gives New Age ideals their power. Many see New Age ideals as a logical necessity. This is why Robert Muller, the Assistant Secretary-General in charge of coordinating 32 specialized agencies and world programs of the UN, has written *New Genesis: The Shaping of a Global Spirituality*. He believes that a united world is not only possible; it is necessary.[54] Many others who recognize these same problems are also working for a united world. Their ideas of a world of unity, love and brotherhood are widely and openly endorsed. Therefore to label the NAM a "mass conspiracy" is not correct.

Even if men could succeed in uniting the world and solving many of its problems, there are two vital issues which are never addressed by humanists and New Agers working for a new world. These are the power of sin within the human heart and the reality of the devil and his power over man's affairs. Both human sin and demonic power are ridiculed and ignored by those who believe that men alone can usher in a New Age. Men who are quite imperfect, indeed who are often evil, and men who in their rejection of God place themselves under the devil's power (II Cor. 4:4) can never achieve a true millennium. Thus, God teaches that some of the ideas for a united world will eventually be used for evil purposes.

For now we believe it is better to limit the use of the word conspiracy to the spiritual realm. The NAM does contain the seeds for a conspiracy, but so have many other movements in history. If at some time America opens itself up to the New Age, and it sweeps the world, then the spiritual powers behind it may take advantage of this movement for more profound purposes. Biblically we know it will be the devil using unsuspecting men as his agents, conspiring behind the scenes to control the world. We also know that one day he will succeed (Rev. 12:9; 13:8,12-17). To what extent the NAM will take part in fulfilling this underworld conspiracy remains to be seen.

24. Is the New Age Movement related to modern psychology?

To varying degrees, certain schools of modern psychology are supportive of New Age philosophy and practice. Some of these schools are the Humanistic, the Jungian, the Transpersonal (stressing Eastern psychologies), and literally scores of unconventional "fringe" psychotherapies. Thus, aspects of psychology are uniting to encourage confidence in the exploration of the mind to bring about the mystical experiences associated with the East and the occult. In fact, many are increasingly viewing psychology as the most promising bridge to the ancient occult wisdom. As they do so, psychology is becoming a principal vehicle for expanding New Age influence in our culture.[55]

25. Is the New Age Movement related to witchcraft and Satanism?

There are similarities between the doctrines of the NAM and witchcraft and Satanism. Although they are by no means identical, there is general agreement among them that "all is one," "all is God," and that we are our own gods. There is also agreement on the personal use of both occult power and the spirit world. And there is an agreement on the rejection of absolute morality, including Christian values.[56]

This is why many witches have stated that they welcome the New Age movement; it not only reflects their views of the world, it also makes it easier for other people to accept witchcraft and to even become witches themselves. Thus, guru Bhagwan Shree Rajneesh states that witchcraft constitutes "one of the greatest possibilities of human growth."[57]

Because of the NAM there is a revival not only of witchcraft but of all forms of occultism in our country, including Satanism. Investigative reporter, Maury Terry, has documented that there exists a Satanic network crisscrossing the nation. This Satanic network has apparently influenced Charles Manson, the "Son of Sam" killer David Berkowitz, and other serial killers—and is responsible for a large number of clandestine murders of innocent persons.[58] Although most New Agers would strongly object to any connection between Satanism and the New Age, even some Satanists recognize there is a connection. Thus, for example, former military Colonel and Satanist, Dr. Michael Aquino, high priest of the church of Set, could say in response to the question "Is Satanism the same as the New Age?", "Yes, but I would say we have a more precise grasp of what it actually is we are looking at here...of what is actually happening here [in the new age]."[59]

Thus, there are connections between the NAM and witchcraft and Satanism even though this fact is not recognized by most people.

Section V
Analysis and Critique

26. What evidence would lead a thinking person to conclude spirit guides are dangerous?

An important question to consider is, even though these spirits appear to be so helpful, kind, and wise, what is the real motive behind their behavior? New Agers firmly believe these spirits are highly advanced spiritual "Masters" who have come to instruct humankind and prepare the way for the coming New Age. Thus, by definition, the NAM believes the teachings of the spirits are good, even divine.

To the contrary, however, we will present evidence to show the teachings of these spirits are not divine. Rather, the teachings of the spirits are immoral, anti-social, un-biblical and prejudiced against Christ. Each thinking person should ask, "Is it logical that good or divine spirits would teach lies?" Men worldwide usually consider Christ as good and His teaching as beneficial. Why would "good" spirits adamantly be opposed to Him and consistently lie about His teachings? It must be admitted that it is at least a possibility that these are not good spirits but evil spirits who are masquerading as helpful beings. Could their real purpose be to appear helpful and give mystical experiences only to deceive men spiritually?

In brief, the evidence demonstrates that these "loving" spirits with their endless disguises (from "angels," to "aliens," to "nature spirits") fit the category of the demonic. It can be shown that these spirits promote sin and immorality, endorse occultism, and some even promote perverse rituals such as necrophilia or sex with corpses.[60] They also pervert and distort Biblical truth, reject Christ and hate the God of

32

the Bible, and purposely deceive those who listen sometimes with sadistic intent.[61] If the above can be demonstrated, as it can, what other conclusions may we arrive at other than these creatures are deceiving spirits?

Consider the teachings of the spirit entity "Emmanuel" as found in the text by Pat Rodegast titled *Emmanuel's Book*. Morally, Emmanuel teaches the permissibility and desirability of divorce (in "incompatible" marriages); the possibility of "open marriage" (adultery); the permissibility of abortion ("a useful act" when done "with willingness to learn" for "nothing in your human world is absolutely wrong"); and homosexuality and bisexuality as normal behavior (even in full recognition of the AIDS plague).[62]

Emmanuel also demeans political leaders as ignorant and sick and teaches that the six million Jews who perished in the Holocaust really chose to be murdered in order to grow spiritually. Thus, Emmanuel says that Hitler and Stalin should not be condemned too severely, for they also are part of God.[63] Are these the kinds of moral codes men should live by? Are they good ethical teachings in any sense? Can they be considered socially constructive? Are these ideas what we would expect from morally pure, divine or highly evolved spiritual beings? Or, on the other hand, are they what we would expect from evil spiritual beings? The fact is that Emmanuel's teachings are not the exception; they are merely representative of thousands of other spirits' teachings in general.

In general all the spirits agree theologically, which is very interesting. Emmanuel, along with other spirits, teaches that God and man are one (see Gen. 1–3); that faith in God is unnecessary (see Heb. 11:1); that Christ is man's "higher self" (see John 3:16,18; Phil. 2:1-9); and that death is "absolutely safe," merely a change without judgment (see John 3:36; Heb. 9:27; Rev. 20:10-25).[64]

Here are some other typical New Age beliefs that Emmanuel and other spirits teach—"all is one," there is no good or evil, cosmic evolution through reincarnation, one-worldism, contact with alleged extraterrestrials, the importance of spirit contact, etc.[65] In light of this evidence, what do you conclude are the motives of the spirits?

27. Are New Age mystical experiences really spiritual traps?

Today there exists a great misunderstanding in the area of psychic phenomena, mystical experiences, and the occult.

They are all viewed as good, progressive and of divine origin. In the future they are expected to be part of the natural and normal aspect of human evolution or potential. These are assumed to be not only "good" but "safe" activities. Usually the harmful realities are learned too late because our society rejects the idea of demonic powers who purposely deceive by masquerading as good.

People in the New Age have no idea that their new spiritual practices may be involving them with demons. For example, Johanna Michaelsen once believed she was serving God and Jesus by working for a psychic surgeon. At times she experienced great joy and peace through her New Age practices. Her spirit guide even claimed to be Jesus. In the process of becoming a Christian she discovered that this spirit guide had purposely deceived her and was a demon. She recalls, "Murderous demonic rage had been the spirits' reaction to my potential decision to accept Jesus Christ of Nazareth as He is, rather than as I had come to think He should be."[66]

Doreen Irvine realized the same truth. As a practicing witch who used psychic powers, she believed they were only part of everyone's "human potential." One day she discovered that the real power came from evil spirits. She came to realize they actually dwelled within her—something she had never known. She observes, "Now I was no stranger to demons. Had I not often called on them to assist me in rites as witch and Satanist? [Now] for the first time I knew these demons were within me, not outside. It was a startling revelation . . . they actually controlled me."[67]

Finally, medium Raphael Gasson said that his spirit helpers tried to kill him when he decided to leave them and turn to Jesus Christ. He states, "As a former Spiritualist minister and active medium, it is possible for me to say that at the time of my participation in the Movement, I actually believed that these spirits were the spirits of the departed dead and that it was my duty to preach this to all those with whom I came into contact day by day. It was my earnest desire that mankind should accept this 'glorious truth' and find joy in the knowledge that there was no death."[68] Yet Gasson went on to say his very own spirit guide "attempted to kill me when it became obvious that I was out to denounce spiritualism."[69]

From this, one can see that initially at least, the New Age convert may encounter many exciting and joyful experiences. This is what the spirits desire to give because they lead people deeper into New Age philosophy and practices.

But once a person is truly "hooked," the picture may change drastically. What New Agers must consider is that they may themselves be part of a spiritual "con." If a swindler is clever enough, his victim will joyfully hand over his entire life savings. It is only too late that he discovers his loss. New Agers are trusting in giving their minds and bodies to spirit beings they know little about. If these spirits are demons, logically what do you think will be the consequences?

28. Where are the ideas of the New Age Movement leading America?

The New Age movement is already having a significant impact on America. This can be seen in the classification of spiritual teachers. Because of the New Age, many are being classified as spiritual leaders and teachers who are really occultists. They are occultists (even if they reject the label) because of their involvement with spirits, who influence and/or control these persons.

The very fact that such leaders typically go through an occult training in the process of becoming leaders; the fact that they are using spiritual (occult) power; the far too numerous admissions of their having spirit guides—these considerations in light of the Biblical data (II Cor. 4:4; Eph. 2:2; I John 5:19) lead us to conclude such religious leaders are spirit-influenced and sometimes demonized.[70]

These teachers are swaying millions of people. What this means is that millions of Americans are being influenced by the very spirits who instruct such teachers. It means our nation is in the process of accepting what the Bible calls demonization and we are doing it on a significant scale.

However, the experience of demonization in America is not necessarily the same as the illustrations of demon possession in the New Testament. Today's Americans enter into these experiences voluntarily and interpret them as having positive spiritual value. A good example of this is people who are practicing channeling. Time and again in the autobiographies of such persons, we discover that the process of spirit possession is an essentially "positive," pleasurable, life-changing and power-inducing experience.[71] This is initially true as the spirits seem to want to make a good impression. In the long run, however, it is another story entirely.

The New Age revival also has brought about cultural, societal and family changes. Ideas have consequences, and philosophies and practices such as the idea that "all is one"

(monism), the rejection of absolute morality, belief in reincarnation and the practices of spirit contact, divination,
psychic development, etc., are changing the way people
treat each other. In addition, it must be remembered that
God judged and destroyed the Canaanite civilization explic-
itly for the idolatrous and occultic practices they had em-
ployed (Deut. 18; Joshua 1–3). In light of this, do you think
America is asking for God's judgment?

29. What should people in the New Age do who are encountering spiritual difficulties?

Spiritual problems have become so widespread that "helping organizations" have been formed to deal with the crises
that are occurring. The spiritual difficulties people are
encountering sends them to New Age counselors.

But the basic problem with New Age counseling is an
incorrect diagnosis of the problem and thus an incorrect
treatment. The concepts of "occult bondage" and demon
possession are not even considered.[72]

In fact, New Age counselors typically encourage the very
occult practices that give birth to the problems. Their fun-
damental premise is that spiritual crises are really part of
each person's spiritual journey and, therefore, something
good. These experiences need not be avoided, they only need
to be handled correctly. In brief, the goal of New Age counseling is to successfully inform and safely integrate these
harmful experiences into a person's life.

What are some of the experiences that New Age counselors are trying to integrate into people's lives? Some people
in the NAM are encountering frightening and unexpected
psychic powers, hallucinations, abrupt possession by spirit
entities, psychic attacks, and the often uncontrollable and
painful kundalini arousal. Others are encountering severe
depression or suicidal tendencies.[73]

In evaluating the problems that come with New Age
practices, two facts are important to consider. First, not one
in a thousand persons in the New Age ever expected to
encounter such alarming experiences. These seekers did
not know that these experiences came with the territory.
Had they known, New Age practices would certainly have
been avoided. Secondly, New Age counseling cannot truly
help a person when it encourages the very ideas and practices that are the source of the problems to begin with.
Because these experiences are occultic and represent contact with demonic powers, the end result of "properly inte-
grating" such experiences may, from a Christian point of

view, be merely a "properly integrated" yet demonized individual who is convinced he is advancing spiritually.

The New Age practitioner who wants deliverance from these problems, who wishes to "turn off" the switch, is left with a dilemma. The New Age has no "off" switch and such a one may be left at the mercy of spirits and forces that will not leave him alone.

Abstinence is the only safe recommendation because occult practices open the doors to demonic deception, manipulation, and possession. Once forbidden practices are engaged in and encountered, a person may only be delivered though the power of the Biblical Jesus Christ. These New Age practices and powers must be renounced (Luke 13:3; James 4:7-8), the sin of involvement repented of and confessed to God (I John 1:9), and Christ must be received as personal Savior and Lord (John 1:12). Any experience of hindrance should be resolved with constant prayer (I Thess. 5:17), Bible study (I Thess. 5:21-22; II Tim. 2:15), and responsible Christian counseling.[74]

30. What does God's Son, Jesus Christ, offer to New Agers looking for answers?

Jesus Christ offers those in the New Age the opportunity to be loved by "the only true God" (John 17:3) and to know and love Him in return.

Everyone wishes to believe in something that in the end will be proven true. The truth that Jesus is God's Son can be proven by Biblical prophecy, by His life and miracles, and by His resurrection from the dead. No other religion or religious leader gives such proof. The New Ager must choose between the New Age and Jesus Christ. The Bible tells us all are sinners and that our sin has separated us from God. Unless we accept God's remedy, that separation will continue on into eternity, which Jesus called hell. But God does not desire that any should perish but that all should come to repentance (II Peter 3:9). Because of His "great love" for us (John 3:16; Rom. 5:8; Eph. 2:4) Christ died to pay for our sin in order that he could forgive us our sin through faith in Him (John 5:24). A part of God's glorious salvation that Jesus Christ offers us is genuine eternal life, not endless reincarnations which promise only more lifetimes of pain and suffering. The Bible says, ". . . God has given us eternal life, and this life is in his Son. He who has the Son has the life; he who does not have the Son of God does not have the life." (I John 5:11-12).

If you are not a Christian, it is eternally important that you make a decision for Jesus Christ with your mind, heart and will.

The Bible teaches:

1. Romans 3:23—All have sinned and fall short of the glory of God.

2. Romans 6:23—The wages of sin is death—eternal separation from God.

3. Romans 6:23—The free gift of God is eternal life provided by the death of Christ on the cross (I Peter 3:18).

4. Luke 13:3—To receive this gift you must be willing to repent; that is to confess you are a sinner and be willing to turn away from the sins of your life and follow Christ.

5. John 1:12—You must receive Christ personally.

Do you desire to know the living God? Are you willing to acknowledge your sin before Him and to receive His Son? If you are, John Stott recommends the following prayer:

> "Lord Jesus Christ, **I humbly acknowledge** that I have sinned in my thinking and speaking in acting, that I am guilty of deliberate wrongdoing, and that my sins have separated me from Your Holy presence, and that I am helpless to commend myself to You;
>
> "**I firmly believe** that You died on the cross for my sins, bearing them in Your own body and suffering in my place the condemnation they deserved;
>
> "**I have thoughtfully counted the cost** of following You. I sincerely repent, turning away from my past sins. I am willing to surrender to You as my Lord and Master. Help me not to be ashamed of You;
>
> "**So now I come to You**. I believe that for a long time You have been patiently standing outside the door knocking. I now open the door. Come in, Lord Jesus, and be my Savior and my Lord forever. Amen."[75]

If you prayed this prayer, there are several things you can do to grow in the Christian life. Start to read a modern translation Bible and find a good church that honors Christ. Tell someone you have just become a Christian so they may pray for you and encourage you in your new life with Christ, for remember, in Christ "are hidden all the treasures of wisdom and knowledge" (Col. 2:3).

NOTES

1. Shirley MacLaine, *Out on a Limb* (New York: Bantam, 1983), p. 268.
2. Robert Lindsay, "Spiritual Concepts Drawing a Different Breed of Adherent," *New York Times*, September 29, 1986, p. 1; Robert Burroughs, "Americans Get Religion in the New Age," *Christianity Today*, May 16, 1986, pp. 1, 17; Douglas Groothuis, *Unmasking of the New Age* (Downers Grove, IL: InterVarsity Press), 1986.
3. From Nina Easton, "Shirley MacLaine's Mysticism for the Masses," *The Los Angeles Times Magazine*, September 6, 1987, p. 33.
4. Ibid.
5. Ibid., p. 8.
6. Brooks Alexander, "Theology From the Twilight Zone," *Christianity Today*, September 18, 1987, p. 22.
7. e.g., *The Los Angeles Times*, October 3, 1986, Part IX, p. 1.
8. *The Los Angeles Times*, August 6, 1986, Part II, p. 1.
9. Kenneth Feder, "Spooks, Spirits, and College Students," *The Humanist*, May-June, 1985.
10. e.g., on scientific mysticism see Dean C. Halverson, "Science: Quantum Physics and Quantum Leaps," in Karen Hoyt and the Spiritual Counterfeits Project, *The New Age Rage* (Old Tappan, NJ: Revell, 1987), pp. 74-90; on the military see Martin Ebon, *Psychic Warfare* (New York: McGraw-Hill, 1983); Ronald McRae, *Mind Wars: The True Story of Secret Government Research Into Military Potential of Psychic Weapons* (New York: St. Martin's Press, 1984). See also The *Spiritual Counterfeits Project Journal*, Vol. 7, no. 1 (P.O. Box 4308, Berkeley, CA, 94704) and Marie Sengler and Brian Van Der Horst, "The Inner Directed," *New Realities*, Vol. 3, no. 6 (1980).
11. Easton, op. cit., p. 10.
12. Ibid, c.f. Elliot Miller, "Channeling: Spiritistic Revelations for the New Age," *Christian Research Journal*, Fall, 1987, p. 14.
13. Easton, op. cit., p. 7.
14. Among his books are *Up From Eden, The Atman Project, No Boundary, Transformations of Consciousness* (ed.) and *The Spectrum of Consciousness*.
15. The best illustration of this is *The Journal of Transpersonal Psychology*, which began in 1969 and is considered the leading journal in the field. The past President of the Association for Transpersonal Psychology, publisher of the Journal, is Dr. Frances Vaughan. She observes, "The transpersonal perspective sees the Eastern spiritual disciplines and Western scientific approaches to psychology as complementary." Frances

Vaughan, "The Transpersonal Perspective: A Personal Overview," *The Journal of Transpersonal Psychology*, Vol. 14, no. 1, p. 37.

16. Walter Truett Anderson, *The Upstart Spring: Esalen and the American Awakening* (Menlo Park, CA: Addison-Wesley, 1983), p. 104.

17. Taken from the televised mini-series "Out on a Limb," 1987.

18. N. Kasturi, *Sathyam-Shivam-Sundaram: The Life of Bhagavan Sri Sathya Sai Baba Part 3* (Brindavan Whitefield, Bangalore, India: Sri Sathya Sai Foundation, 1973), p. 112.

19. Bhagwan Shree Rajneesh, "I am the Messiah Here and Now," *Sannyas* Magazine, No. 5 (September-October), 1978, p. 34; Rajneesh, *The Book of the Secrets*, Vol. 1 (San Francisco: Harper & Row, 1974), p. 22.

20. Rajneesh in Swami Anand Yarti, *The Sound of Running Water: A Photobiography of Bhagwan Shree Rajneesh and His Work, 1974-1978* (Poona, India, Poona Rajneesh Foundation, 1980), p. 382.

21. Vivekananda in Swami Nikhilananda (compiler), *Vivekananda The Yogas and Other Works* (New York: Ramabrishna-Vivekananda Center, 1953), Rev., p. 530.

22. Ibid.

23. Rajneesh, *The Book of the Secrets*, Vol. 1, p. 399. Rajneesh is explaining spiritual wisdom to Arjuna, the warrior in the *Bhagavad Gita*.

24. e.g., "Seth's" views on reconstructing psychology along New Age lines in Jane Roberts', *The Nature of Human Personality* (1974); *Adventures in Consciousness: An Introduction to Aspect Psychology* (1975); and *Psychic Politics: An Aspect Psychology Book* (1976).

25. Stanislav Grof (ed.), *Ancient Wisdom and Modern Science* (New York: State University of New York Press, 1984), esp. pp. V-XXXI; 3-31.

25a. For example, consider a statement on the back cover of *The Eye of Shiva: Eastern Mysticism and Science* (New York: William Morrow, 1981), "Amaury de Riencourt maintains that the 'higher state of consciousness' of the meditating yogi, the 'enlightenment' of Eastern mysticism, is not a dream state but a true description of reality. He believes that this consciousness, symbolized by the Eye of Shiva, can provide the appropriate model for further research in physics. Furthermore, he argues that this 'hidden level of existence' can unite Eastern and Western traditions and end forever the dualisms of Western thought."

26. John Ferguson, *An Illustrated Encyclopedia of Mysticism and the Mystery Religions* (New York: Seabury Press, 1977), p. 148; Brad Steiger, *Revelation: The Divine Fire* (1973); Walter Pahnke, "Implications of L.S.D. and Experimental Mysticism," in Charles Tart (ed.), *Altered States of Consciousness* (New York: Wiley and Sons, 1969), pp. 399-428; Robert Crookall, *The Interpretation of Cosmic and Mystical Experience* (Cambridge: James Clark & Co., 1969); W. T. Stace, *Mysticism and Philosophy* (New York: Macmillan, 1960); R. M. Bucke, *Cosmic Consciousness* (New York: E. P. Dutton, 1901); Lawrence LeShan, *Toward a General Theory of the Paranormal* (New York: Parapsychology Foundation, 1969).

27. The first major text on "channeling" discussing these and other entities from a New Age perspective is Jon Klimo, *Channeling: Investigations on Receiving Information from Paranormal Sources* (Los Angeles: Jeremy P. Tarcher, 1987).

28. Lynn Smith, "The New Chic Metaphysical Fad of Channeling," *Los Angeles Times*, December 5, 1986, Part V, c.f. Katherine Lowry, "Channelers: Mouthpieces of the Spirits," *Omni* Magazine, October, 1987.

29. e.g., Laeh Garfield, *Companions in Spirit: A Guide to Working With Your Spirit Helpers* (Berkeley, CA: Celestial Arts, 1984); Robin Westen, *Channelers: A New Age Directory* (New York: Putnam, 1988); Roman and Packer, *Opening to Channel: How to Connect with Your Guide* (H.J. Kramer, 1987); Cathryn Ridle *Channeling: How to Reach Out to Your Spirit Guides* (Bantam, 1988).

30. See also *Metapsychology: The Journal of Discarnate Intelligence.*

31. Lowry, op. cit., p. 22.

32. Alexander, op. cit., p. 22.

33. This was a national poll conducted by the University of Chicago's National Opinion Research Council; see the report in Andrew Greeley, "Mysticism Goes Mainstream," *American Health*, January-February, 1987.

34. Lowry, op. cit.

35. Carol Ostrom, "Pastor Resigns, Sticks with Disputed Belief" in *The Seattle Times*, July 28, 1986, Part B.

36. For a critique of *God Calling* see Edmond Gruss, "A Critical Look at a Christian Best Seller," *Personal Freedom Outreach Newsletter*, Vol. 6, no. 3 (P.O. Box 26062, St. Louis, MO 63136). The "Evangelical Christian Publishers Association Bestsellers" list, reported in *Christianity Today*, February 19, 1988, p. 2, lists it as number 10 on the paperback list.

37. See *Time Magazine*, November 13, 1972, and *New Realities*, Richard Bach Interview, November-December, 1984, p. 56. Bach was also indebted to "Seth."

38. See p. 9 in the critique of channeling in the *Spiritual Counterfeits Project Journal*, Vol. 7, no. 1 (P.O. Box 4308, Berkeley, CA, 1987).

39. See "Agartha: Journey to the Stars," and Mentor, "Man as God: Learning to Channel," in *Holistic Life Magazine*, Summer, 1985, p. 22.

40. Collectively the NAM is a combination of related pantheistic beliefs: 1) monism, the belief that all true reality is divine, with the corollary that the phenomenal universe is outwardly an illusion (maya) but inwardly divine in its true essence; 2) panentheism, the belief that the universe is God's "body" and so God is more than the physical universe; 3) pantheism, the belief that the physical universe is God.

41. See Walter Martin, *Kingdom of the Cults* (Minneapolis: Bethany, 1987) and Walter Martin (ed.), *The New Cults* (Santa Ana: Vision House, 1984).

42. e.g., David Fetcho, "David Fetcho's Story: Last Meditation/Lotus Adept," *Spiritual Counterfeits Project Special Collection Journal*, Winter, 1984, p. 33.

43. Rajneesh, *I Am the Gate* (San Francisco: Perennial Library, 1978), p. 16.

44. Napolean Hill, *Grow Rich with Peace of Mind* (New York: Ballantine, 1982), pp. 158, 160.

45. e.g., his *Positive Imaging* (New York: Ballantine, 1983).

46. Robert Schuller, *Peace of Mind Through Possibility Thinking* (New York: Jove/Berkeley, 1985), pp. 130-138.

47. K. Bottomly, J. French, "Christians Meditate, Too," *Yoga Journal*, May-June, 1984, pp. 26-28, 48.

48. See E. S. Gallegos "Animal Imagery, the Chakra System and Psychotherapy," *The Journal of Transpersonal Psychology*— Vol. 15, no. 2.

49. See David Benner (ed.), *Baker Encyclopedia of Psychology* (1985), under these listings. See also under "transpersonal psychology," "psychosynthesis," "bioenergetics," and "hypnosis."

50. For an analysis of these and other topics see Reisser, Reisser and Weldon, *New Age Medicine* (Chattanooga, TN: Global, 1988).

51. Ibid., ch. 9.

52. See Clifford Wilson and John Weldon, *Psychic Forces*, (Chattanooga, TN: Global), Section III.

53. Robert Muller in *New Genesis: Shaping a Global Spirituality* (New York: Doubleday, 1984), discusses several of these. See Peter Russell, *The Global Brain: Speculations on the Evolutionary Leap to Planetary Consciousness* (Los Angeles: J. P. Tarcher, 1983), and Daisaku Ikeda, *The Toynbee-Ikeda Dialogue* (1976), p. 243.

54. Muller, op. cit., pp. 47-49, 89-90, 120-127.

55. This is the view of New Age cultural commentator Theodore Rozak, in *The Unfinished Animal* (New York: Harper & Row, 1977), pp. 17-18; see Charles Tart (ed.), *Transpersonal Psychologies* (New York: Harper & Row, 1977); Seymour Boorstein (ed.), *Transpersonal Psychotherapy* (Palo Alto, CA: Science and Behavior Books, Inc., 1980); Alta J. LaDage, *Occult Psychology: A Comparison of Jungian Psychology and the Modern Quabalah* (St. Paul, MN: Llewellyn, 1978); John Levy "Transpersonal Psychology and Jungian Psychology" and Shawn Steggles et. al., "Gestalt Therapy and Eastern Philosophies: A Partially Annotated Bibliography," *Journal of Humanistic Psychology*, Spring 1983; Carl Rogers, *A Way of Being* (Boston: Houghton Mifflin Co., 1980), pp. 82-92, 100-102, 129-132, 253-256, 312-315, 343-352; Richard D. Mann, *The Light of Consciousness: Explorations in Transpersonal Psychology* (Albany: State University of New York Press, 1984); Roger Walsh, et. al., *Beyond Ego: Transpersonal Dimensions in Psychology* (Los Angeles: J. P. Tarcher, 1980).

56. e.g., Margot Adler, *Drawing Down the Moon: Witches, Druids, Goddess-Worshippers, and other Pagans in America Today* (New York: Viking Press, 1979), pp. 21-29, 58, 64, 95-113, 150-154, 385; Maury Terry, *The Ultimate Evil: An Investigation of America's Most Dangerous Satanic Cult* (Garden City, NY: Dolphin, 1987), pp. XI-XIII; 499-512; Carl A. Raschke, "Satanism and the Devolution of the New Religions," *Spiritual Counterfeits Project Newsletter*, Vol. 11, no. 3, pp. 22-29.

57. Yarti, op. cit., p. 364.

58. Terry, op. cit., pp. xi-xiii; 499-512.

59. As stated on the Oprah Winfrey Show, February 17, 1988.

60. Mircea Eliade, *Occultism, Witchcraft and Cultural Fashions* (Chicago: University of Chicago Press, 1976), p. 71; Tal Brooke, *Riders of the Cosmic Circuit* (Batavia, IL: Lion, 1986), pp. 199-208.

61. Mary Lutyens, *Krishnamurtii: The Years of Awakening* (New York: Avon, 1976), p. 203.

62. Pat Rodegast, *Emmanuel's Book* (Weston, CT: Friends Press, 1986), pp. 132, 198-199, 200, 201, 227, 232, 205, 161.

63. Ibid., pp. 228, 208, XX, 145, 223, 151, 88.

64. Ibid., pp. 39, 29, 33, 30, 42, 44, 243, 169-172.

65. Ibid., pp. 138, XIX, 142-143, 153, 222, 239-241, 72, 74, 76-77, 78.

66. Johanna Michaelsen, *The Beautiful Side of Evil* (Eugene, OR: Harvest House, 1982), p. 148.

67. Doreen Irvine, *Freed From Witchcraft* (Nashville, TN: Thomas Nelson, 1973), pp. 123-126.

68. Raphael Gasson, *The Challenging Counterfeit* (Plainfield, NJ: Logos, 1970), p. 36.

69. Ibid., p. 83.

70. Many spiritual teachers or leaders admit their occultic training e.g., Paul Twitchell in *The Flute of God* (San Diego: Illuminated Way Press, 1975), p. 118 and Brad Steiger, *In My Soul I Am Free* (San Diego: Illuminated Way Press) n.d., pp. 82-83; Werner Erhard, founder of est in W. W. Bartley, *Werner Erhard, The Transformation of a Man: The Founding of est* (New York: Clarkson N. Porter, 1978), pp. 14, 37, 75-76, 81-82, 118-119, 145, 148, 158. Autobiographies of such leaders often reveal such involvement e.g., for Jose Silva, founder of Silva Mind Control, *I Have a Hunch: The Autobiography of Jose Silva* (Laredo, TX: Institute of Psycho-orientology, 1983), chs. 10, 17, 21, 23, 29; for Earlyne Chaney, co-founder of Astara, *Remembering: The Autobiography of a Mystic* (Los Angeles: Astara, 1974), chs. 9-16; Paraamahansa Yogananda, founder of the Self-Realization Fellowship, *Autobiography of a Yogi* (Los Angeles: Self Realization Fellowship, 1973), chs. 14, 43.

71. See Malachi Martin, *Hostage to the Devil* (New York: Bantam, 1980) for examples.

72. See Kurt Koch, *Occult Bondage and Deliverance* (Grand Rapids, MI: Kregel, 1970); John Warwick Montgomery (ed.), *Demon Possession* (Minneapolis, MN: Bethany, 1976).

73. See Martin Ebon (ed.), *The Satan Trap: Dangers of the Occult* (Garden City, NY: Doubleday, 1976) and Emma Bragdon, *A Sourcebook for Helping People in Spiritual Emergency*, 1987, part of her Ph.D. dissertation of the same title on record at the Institute for Transpersonal Psychology in Menlo Park, CA.

74. See Koch, op. cit., and for the counseling professional his *Christian Counseling and Occultism* (Grand Rapids, MI: Kregel, 1972).

75. John Stott, *Becoming A Christian* (Downers Grove, IL: InterVarsity, 1950), pp. 25-26.

RECOMMENDED READING

Groothuis, Douglas R., *Unmasking the New Age*, InterVarsity, 1986.

Hoyt, Karen, and the Spiritual Counterfeits Project, *The New Age Rage*, Fleming H. Revell, 1987.

North, Gary, *Unholy Spirits*, Dominion Press, 1987.

Reisser, Paul and Teri, and Weldon, John, *New Age Medicine*, Global, 1988.

Hunt, Dave, *The Seduction of Christianity*, Harvest House, 1986.

Brooke, Tal, *Riders of the Cosmic Circuit*, Lion, 1986.

Schaeffer, Francis, *True Spirituality*, Tyndale, 1976.

Weldon, John, and Levitt, Zola, *Psychic Healing: An Expose of an Occult Phenomenon*, Moody Press, 1982.

Wilson, Clifford, and Weldon, John, *Psychic Forces and Occult Shock,* Global, 1986.

Geisler, Norman L., and Watkins, William D., *Perspectives: Understanding and Evaluating Today's World Views*, Here's Life Publishers, 1984.

Raschke, Carl A., *The Interruption of Eternity: Modern Gnosticism and the Origins of the New Religious Consciousness*, Nelson-Hall, 1980.

Stalker, Douglas, and Glymour, Clark, *Examining Holistic Medicine,* Prometheus Books, 1985.

Elliott Miller, "Channeling: Spiritistic Revelations for the New Age," part one, *Christian Research Journal*, Fall, 1987, pp. 9-15.

Pement, Eric, *The 1988 Directory of Cult Research Organizations*, Chicago, IL, Cornerstone Press, 1988.

Wilson, Clifford, and Weldon, John, *Close Encounters: A Better Explanation*, Master Books, 1978.

"For Additional Information"

The following organizations can provide additional information on a variety of New Age philosophies, religions, trends and phenomena.

1. Spiritual Counterfeits Project, P. O. Box 4308, Berkeley, CA 94704. Their order number is 415-540-0300. Their information

hotline number is 415-540-5767 (Monday and Wednesday 10 A.M.—2 P.M. Pacific Time).

2. Christian Research Institute, P. O. Box 500, San Juan Capistrano, CA 92693-0500; phone number 714-855-9926.

3. The Skeptical Inquirer (Committee for the Scientific Investigation of the Claims of the Paranormal, 3159 Bailey Avenue, Buffalo, New York 14215-0229.) Although this organization writes from a largely rationalistic perspective, its journal contains a number of helpful critiques and analyses of many New Age phenomena and philosophies.